SLAYING
THE LUST
DRAGON

Todd Friel

Ridgeway Publishing
Medina, New York

SLAYING THE LUST DRAGON

*To obtain additional copies
please visit your local
bookstore or contact:*
Ridgeway Publishing
3161 Fruit Ave.
Medina, NY 14103
ph: (888) 822-7894
fax: (585) 798-9016

ISBN# 978-099066553-3

Printed in the United States of America

SLAYING
THE LUST
DRAGON

Todd Friel

A NOTE FROM THE PUBLISHER

We found Todd Friel's sermon on killing pornography to be inspiring and motivating. After being approached by others to transcribe and publish this work into book form, we consented and we trust you will be blessed.

Because this was a preached message, you will notice the content reads a bit differently from an intentional writing. We tried to edit lightly for clarity and readability but still maintain the preached style.

We want to extend gratitude to Burning Bush Communications for extending kind permission and co-operation in this project. May God receive all the glory and we pray many souls can be delivered from this snare of the devil—the curse of pornography.

PRELUDE

There is no denying that the feminist movement has been wildly successful at softening most men in our metro-sexualized society. That claim can be substantiated with just two words: One Direction.

Even Christian men are not exempt from the pressure to use moisturizer and eye cream. Unfortunately, the evangelical response to the feminization of America hasn't been anything to cheer about.

Rather than running to the Bible for guidance, ministries dedicated to getting men to man up encourage grown men to shoot wild animals, climb mountains, and go whitewater rafting. These are perfectly fine activities, but they are hardly the stuff that constitutes Biblical manhood.

What does the Bible say makes for a Godly man? There are many things, but for this discussion, we are going to define Biblical manhood as the ability to master our own passions so we can be the best husband, the best father, and the best follower of Jesus Christ possible.

True manliness is doing the hard lifting of examining yourself to see where you might have some flaws, some foibles, and some faults, so that they can be corrected and you can be a better Christian, husband and daddy. Now those are manly things. By reading this book that's exactly what you're endeavoring to do.

Way to go, Sir. You are a man who is striving to be please your God and endeavoring to be a better follower of the Lord Jesus.

I do not present this from a lofty position. Lust is every man's battle. It is an issue that every man needs to mortify and I applaud you for your willingness to do some heavy lifting.

A HIGHER CALLING

There are two titles for this message. The first title is: "A Higher Calling." The second title is called: "The Most Uncomfortable 40 Minutes of Your Life." The title you prefer will depend on how you respond to a sermon focusing on the scourge of the modern church: Internet pornography.

You may be thinking that doesn't seem like an appropriate topic to discuss in church. If that is true I would like to submit to you then, the Bible is inappropriate because the Bible does indeed address sex and marriage and intimate relationships. If you have read the Song of Solomon, you know it does so in a rather unapologetic fashion.

Furthermore, sex is good. It is God's intention and plan for many great reasons and to talk about sexual issues as if it's a shameful thing really is to say, "Your intention and plan isn't very good, God."

The fact that you and I tend to blush when the subject of sex is raised is more of a testimony to our corrupt nature than it is to the issue itself.

Can you imagine if I brought up the subject of waxed beans; nobody would walk out of church saying, "That is so inappropriate." Sex, in and of itself, is no more sinful than waxed beans.

Why then do we blush when the subject of sex is addressed? Because we have so corrupted it that we tend to think that sex is dirty in any context.

Sex is not dirty; it is what we do to it that makes it dirty. Paul does not hesitate to admonish us for mishandling God's good gift. And we should not plug our ears because our hearing is tainted by our own presuppositions about intimacy.

Finally, to not address this awkward topic would be a disservice to the millions of men and women who are affected by the issue of pornography. Not only does this sin affect us temporarily, it can also affect us eternally.

1 Corinthians 6 tells us that there is no sin that's so affects the body as sexual immorality. 1 Corinthians 6 also says all fornicators; all adulterers will have their part in a lake of fire. That alone should motivate us to push pass the awkwardness and tackle an issue that

has eternal consequences.

1 Timothy 1:10 says that fornicators will have their part in a lake of fire. James 1: 15 says that sin, when it comes to its fullest form, leads to death. This is not a peripheral issue, this is not a spiritual discipline, this is a matter of life and death and if you do not kill pornography in your life, it will kill you. Count on it.

A BIG PROBLEM

How pervasive is the sin of pornography? Brace yourself for these statistics.

"Focus on The Family" invited pastors to confess, "Have you, within the last month, intentionally gone to a pornographic site to view pornography?" Over 30% said "Yes." Those are the shepherds. What are the sheep doing?

According to Pure Life Ministries, 68% of evangelical men admit to viewing pornography on a regular basis. Pure Life Ministries discovered that 50% of pastors regularly view porn.

This is a huge, huge problem. Pornography is the seventh largest industry in our country. We must address it, as uncomfortable as it might be.

Slaying the Lust Dragon

Slaying the Lust Dragon

FOR THE LADIES

L adies, as we begin, perhaps you are not convinced so many men are consuming filth. You need to know something; I don't know that we can preach on it long enough, or that we can explain it clearly enough—we men are built so..., uh, well, we're different than you. But in this area, we are radically different from you.

Without your restraining influence and the restraining influence of the Holy Spirit pulling us back in this area, we would all swim in the mire of sexual debauchery.

Let me make my case; consider homosexuality. Statistics say that homosexuals will have between 1,500 and 2,000 partners in their lifetime. Why do gay men act that way? They don't have your influence.

You aren't pulling them back. The Holy Spirit isn't in them, restraining them and growing them in holiness, there's no commitment, there's no courtship, there is no standard. Gay men have hundreds of partners because other gay men are only interested in the physical act. That would be true of heterosexual men if it weren't for you and the Holy Spirit.

As long as we are talking to the ladies, I would like to take a moment to address something that can be easily misunderstood: the modesty issue. Ladies, I would ask you, as sisters in Christ, to please be mindful about your apparel.

There are few analogies more trite than the one you are about to hear. If you knew a friend was trying to kick the smoking habit, would you light up a Viceroy and blow the smoke in her face?

Trust me when I say that wearing tight and skin-bearing apparel is far more tempting than smelling the smoke from a cigarette. We are not Muslims; we don't want you to wear burqas. But if you want to help your Christian brother not stumble, then please dress in a way that shows your love, not your body.

If you're thinking, "Well pal, that's just your sin." You're right, it is our sin if we look and go beyond temptation into sin by lusting, you are correct, it is our sin.

But there is another sin involved here if you lead

us into temptation. So please, don't be guilty of that sin and you'll be doing us a great, big favor by not dressing in a way that leads us beyond temptation into sin.

Now there are two groups of women I'd like to address before we turn to the men. To the first group of women: you are devastated right now. You are just absolutely broken because you know that your husband is involved in some way, shape or form with pornography. You know it and your heart is absolutely broken.

Can I just tell you something? First of all, "I'm so sorry." But second of all, "You've got to know, it has nothing to do with you. If your husband is using a computer to look up xxx rated sites, that's his sin. And his sin is not your fault, it has nothing to do with you, with the way you look, how much you weigh, how much money you have or what you do for a living. It has nothing to do with you! It is his sin! Do not put that burden on yourself!

There's a second group of women. You're sitting here and you're thinking, "Not my husband." Well, let me tell you something, lady, praise God! I mean it. Praise God, praise God that you've got a husband who God has changed, radically changed and moved from lust and temptation into a walk of holiness.

May I encourage you today to pray for those

women who don't have the blessing that you and your husband have? We need to pray for them during this service that something might be heard by those men that might change them.

GENTLEMEN

Sir, you need to know that if you are looking at porn, your wife knows. You also need to know that you are crushing her. You have taken a little girl's dream of marrying Prince Charming and you have turned it into a nightmare.

When you said, "I do," she looked in your eyes with hope and trust. She believed you would protect her from perverted men. And you have become the very man she feared.

Have you no compassion? Have you no self-control? Have you no love for her? Have you no desire to be faithful to the vow you made?

If you are looking at porn, you are degrading not just your wife, but your mother, your sisters and every woman in the world.

You are playing the bully and taking advantage of women who are being taken advantage of by a male dominated industry dominated by perverse men.

Instead of being a strong man who sacrifices his life for women and children, you push your way to the front of the line and demand you get what you want no matter who pays the price.

God has higher aspirations for you: you are made to be a hero, a protector, a provider, a leader, a man. When you look at porn, you are not acting like a man; you are acting like a punk.

It's time to play the man. Let's be done with it today for ever! I mean, never again. And I want to suggest a way to do that. A way that will be so pleasing to God, that will so glorify Him and that will change you as a follower of Jesus Christ and as a man and a husband and a father. Ready?

WHAT IS THE POINT?

Rather than looking at sex as a forbidden fruit, I would like to raise your eyes and your view of intimacy so you desire something loftier than mere physical pleasure.

I would like to call you to a picture of what God has done through creation and marriage and the gift of sex and the gift of one another and what it is supposed to accomplish. Understanding that should move us to say, "That is a better goal and desire than looking at filth. Why would I look at something so low when I could participate in something so high and noble? Lord, I will never set my eyes on trash when you are offering me a banquet. I will never look at those forbidden, filthy images again because You are too great and You are too good!"

Let me call you to that today, because He is an amazing God who has done amazing things and when we rightly understand His plan, only a fool would want to deviate from it and bring shame to His name. And I want to do that by taking a look at what marriage is and what God calls you to participate in.

Genesis chapter 2:18-24. "And the Lord God said, It is not good for the man to be alone."

Now note, this is the first time that God said "it's not good." Day one, it's good. Day two it's good, days three, four and five, it's good. But man being alone, that's not good. So God customized a helper suitable for us, literally, a helper corresponding to men. Please note:

1. God did not make a buddy for us. Nothing is wrong with having pals, but the best companion for us is not another guy; it is woman. Play hoops with the fellas, go fishing with your buds, but when it comes to doing

life, the best companion for us is a woman.

2. While man can certainly survive alone, we are BETTER with a woman.

3. A woman helps us in many ways (making a warm home, raising children who love the Lord, taking care of us), but she actually helps us be what we are supposed to be. She calls us to something higher.

4. We cannot have children without a woman.

5. Intimacy cannot be fully enjoyed alone.

Victor Hamilton points out the last part of Genesis 2:18 suggests that what God creates for Adam will correspond to him. So in other words, the help for us is neither superior nor inferior; the woman corresponds to the man.

Men and women are equal in the eyes of the Lord in respect to their nature (Galatians 3:28). God loves men and women equally, but that is not to suggest that men and women do not differ in two very distinct ways:

1. Abilities: men do some things better than women and vice-versa.

2. Roles: God assigned different primary tasks to men and women.

In other words, we compliment one another. As the South Pole is to the North Pole, so it is with man and woman.

The man leads, the woman helps. Before anyone panics, it is not degrading to be a helper. The Hebrew word for helper or helpmeet is: EHZER, coming from the verb AWZAR which means to save from danger or to deliver from debt. Women literally deliver us from the debt of loneliness. It is not good for us to be alone and you rescue us from that loneliness.

Her uniqueness brings completeness to the union. And should anyone be inclined to think that the role of women is inferior to the role of man, it should be noted that God calls Himself the EHZER of Israel. Certainly God is not inferior to Israel, nor is woman inferior to man.

When we are tempted to think that subordination makes one party greater than the other, we need to remember that God the Son submits to God the Father; and Jesus most certainly is not less than the Father.

While women play the subordinate role, that does not give man license to dominate and turn them into play toys, which is precisely what pornography does.

Genesis 2 continues: verse 21, "And the Lord God caused a deep sleep to fall upon Adam, and he slept:" By the way, the Bible never indicates that God pulled us out of that sleep, "and he took one of his ribs, and closed up the flesh instead thereof;" Now the word "rib", well, a lot of our translations say that, but literally it means "side."

This is another indication of equality: God didn't take women from our head, which would mean men are superior. He didn't take you from our feet which, would mean women inferior, but from our side. Women are our equal. "And the rib, which the Lord God had taken from man, made he a woman, and brought her unto the man."

In verse 23 we now get to hear the first recorded words of any man in history. And guess what they are? They're celebratory words for women. This was Adam's covenant vow and it's a celebration of who women are and what they bring to us. Listen carefully; see if any of these phrases sound remotely familiar.

Verse 23, "The man said, This is now bone of my bones, and flesh of my flesh."

Adam used covenant language to define his relationship with woman. These are the same words and concepts that we use in wedding ceremonies today. Bones—strength, flesh—weakness. This was a, if you will, an "in sickness and in health, in strength and in weakness" covenant vow that Adam was making.

Each part of the one flesh relationship was a compliment to the other; physically, spiritually, mentally, sexually. Each of us brings fulfillment to the unfulfilled and a balance to the shortcomings that the other one might have.

Verse 23, "She shall be called Woman, because she was taken out of Man."

The Hebrew word for man is EESH; the Hebrew word for woman is ISH-SHA. To understand the meaning of these words is to further understand our roles. The word ISH- SHA means: soft. Women are soft in at least five ways:

1. They are softer physically.

2. They are softer in their nature.

3. They are softer in their behavior.

4. They are softer in their job responsibilities.

5. They bring a softening to the man who is the hard one.

What is the best thing for a man? A soft, flesh and blood woman. It is not a buddy, it is not ourselves, and it is not an Internet device!

Notice, God did not make multiple women for one man.

Notice, God did not make a computer for a man.

Notice, God did not make a hologram for a man.

A woman, one woman is what's best for us and we're going to see exactly why God designed it that way.

Genesis 2:24, "Therefore shall a man leave his father and his mother, and shall cleave unto his wife:"

Covenant language is still being used here. The word "to leave" is the same word that is used of Israel when she would break her covenant relationship with God.

A man is supposed to break his temporary covenant with his parents and form a lifelong covenant with his bride.

"To cleave", "to cement to" was covenant language meaning: You come together and you are supposed to stay together. The language here is covenantal language intended to cement a lifelong commitment; hence, 'til death do us part.

"And you shall become one flesh." That is why your minister probably talked about two becoming one on your wedding day. Individual parts come together to make a better whole, including sexual completeness.

Being single is like a desk without a chair, a sky without stars, an ocean without fish. While it's nice by itself, it's better together and that is exactly what

God intended for man and woman. To come together and be complete, to be whole.

When you look at pornography, you are corrupting God's plan in several ways:

1. You tell God that His plan for you is not sufficient.

2. You tell the world that God's plan is not sufficient.

3. You tell your covenant partner that she is not sufficient.

4. You are violating what is intended to be a faithful, lifelong, 'til death do you part contract.

But wait, you do something even worse when you violate your marriage covenant by looking at pornography. Much worse.

Let's take a look at the New Testament explanation for what marriage is supposed to be. God could have just had us shack up, but He didn't. He created the institution of marriage to be something far more profound.

There are a lot of reasons for marriage; companionship, procreation, intimacy, help. But here is the supreme reason for marriage and this might be the thing, Sir, that helps you, once and for all, kill pornography.

Ephesians chapter 5:22-32:

> Wives, submit yourselves unto your own husbands, as unto the Lord. For the husband is the head of the wife, even as Christ is the head of the church: and he is the savior of the body. Therefore as the church is subject unto Christ, so let the wives be to their own husbands in every thing.

> Husbands, love your wives, even as Christ also loved the church, and gave himself for it; That he might sanctify and cleanse it with the washing of water by the word, That he might present it to himself a glorious church, not having spot, or wrinkle, or any such thing; but that it should be holy and without blemish. So ought men to love their wives as their own bodies. He that loveth his wife loveth himself. For no man ever yet hated his own flesh; but nourisheth and cherisheth it, even as the Lord the church: For we are members of his body, of his flesh, and of his bones.

Now here comes a reference back to Genesis 2. "For this cause shall a man leave his father and mother, and shall be joined unto his wife, and they two shall be one flesh." Then comes the punch line. "This is a great mystery: but I speak concerning

Christ and the church."

Do you know what marriage is? It is God's great big cosmic play. It is a play called, "The Gospel." And guess who gets to play a role in this play? You and your wife.

Sir, you play the role of Jesus. Tell me that isn't awesome. Madam, you play the role of the church. Together we are supposed to submit one to another so that the world will see our relationship and understand the Gospel. As we play the role of Jesus and the church, the world should be able to look in our windows and conclude, "Oh, that is what it's like to be in a right relationship with Jesus Christ. I see. Look at how he loves her! That's how Jesus loves His church. Look at how she returns his love. That must be what it's like to be a Christian."

Shakespeare almost had it right; all the world is a Gospel stage and you and your wife play a part.

How are you playing your role? Does the world see you and think, "That Jesus, He sure loves!" Or do they see you in front of your computer and go, "Oh, oh, he's into pornography? Jesus does that?"

When you look at pornography, you are corrupting the picture that God intends to paint with your marriage. You tell the world that Jesus isn't pure. You tell the world that Jesus isn't faithful. You tell the world that the Gospel is not worth living for.

The cosmic play continues into the future. I Corinthians 15 describes the consummation of the marriage between Jesus and the church. At a time of God's own choosing, Jesus will return to judge the world and God the Father will gather the elect to present us as a gift to the Bridegroom, Jesus Christ.

But Jesus is going to take the Father's gift (you and me), and return it to the Father that He might be all in all. How dare we corrupt any element of marriage and sully what God intends to be a beautiful picture of His love for the world?

If you truly grasp what God has done for you and is planning to do for you, you will strive to play your role in a way that best represents Him.

Let's take a moment to ponder your options for intimacy: you can stare at a computer screen and do the filthy thing you do, or you can play your role of faithfully, sacrificially loving your bride. You can slink and crawl in the mud; or you can glorify God and magnify His goodness by playing the role of the Lord Jesus Christ.

Do you see how God has something higher, more noble planned for you? He wants to use you for something great. He wants to use you for something cosmic. He wants to use you for something noble.

And there you sit in front of a computer or in a corner clutching a smutty magazine.

You sit there, looking and drooling like a dog in heat when He calls you to glorify Him. Instead, you choose to soil, dirty and shame His great name.

BECOMING OBEDIENT

Now that you have been sufficiently shamed, let's talk about how you can not only be obedient, but *desire* to be obedient and never play the part of the wretch instead of playing the role of Jesus.

Let's go back to the garden and burrow down into why it is not good for man to be alone...sexually.

Men, when it comes to intimacy, we focus pretty much on one thing; the physical aspect of sex. Women on the other hand focus on something different; the emotional aspect.

Physical all by itself: deficient. Emotional all by itself: deficient. Put the two together and it's whole, it's complete. When opposite sex fleshes come together in the intimate act of sex, the emotional and the physical should find their fulfillment.

In order for the woman to fully appreciate the physical aspect of sex, she needs a man. For a man to fully appreciate the emotional aspect of sex, we need a woman.

Now here is the problem with pornography. Pornography says, "No, all alone. All alone." Instead of giving of yourself emotionally to another person who needs you to make her complete, you focus selfishly, and shallowly, on yourself. That is hardly acting like Jesus.

Pornography is contrary to God's amazing plan for fulfillment because pornography is exclusively about physical pleasure, in a selfish way that leads to, mark this well, the corruption of marriage, the corruption of self, the corruption of your family, and it shames the name of your God.

While pornography corrupts you, intimacy with your wife, rightly performed, will make you a better man. Dr. Al Mohler explains this well.

The emotional aspect of sex cannot be divorced from the physical dimension of the act. And a woman has every right to expect that her husband will earn access to the marriage bed. A husband owes his wife the confidence, affection, and emotional support that would lead her to freely give herself to her husband in that act.

God's gift of sexuality is inherently designed to

pull us men out of ourselves toward our spouse. For men this means that marriage calls us out of our self-focused concern for physical pleasure only and toward the totality of the sex act within the marital relationship. God means for a man to be civilized, directed, and stimulated toward marital faithfulness by the fact that his wife will freely give herself to him only when he presents himself as worthy of her attention and desire.

A husband who looks forward to sex with his wife will aim his life toward those things that will bring rightful pride to her heart. He will direct himself to her with love as the foundation of their relationship and will present himself to her as a man in whom she can take both pride and satisfaction. The sex act then becomes a fulfillment of their entire relationship, not an isolated physical act that is merely incidental to their love for each other, but a fulfillment of it.

Do you see? Do you see what it does? That drive that we have, focused rightly, forces us to be a better husband. We want the prize of sex. But because she is so emotionally driven we are forced to behave better in order to earn that prize.

Is God brilliant? I mean, really, do you understand what He has done so that we can be better men? He created us, women and sex so we don't act like the dogs that we're inclined to be.

The Christian man should never hope to "get lucky." He should play the man who earns it. That is what God is calling you to do: focus on your winning your wife's affection and you and your wife and your children will be better for it and God will be glorified.

"Now, consider another man," says Mohler.

"Pornography is the essence of his interest. Rather than taking satisfaction in his wife, he looks at dirty pictures in order to be rewarded with arousal that comes without responsibility, without expectation, without demand. This man need not be concerned with his physical appearance, his personal hygiene or his moral character in the eyes of a wife. He faces no requirement of personal respect and no eyes gaze upon him in order to evaluate the seriousness and worthiness of his sexual desire."

If you are looking at porn, you are not a man; at least you are not the man you could be. God is calling you to something higher, and He wants to use your healthy sexual drive to mature and grow you. And He will, if you will aim it in the right direction; toward your wife.

Pornography, like all sin, lies. Porn tells you that your computer is better than your wife. That is a lie. Stop listening to lies and start listening to truth: you can be a better man if you stop looking at porn and start earning your wife's affection.

All of your affection, all of it, give it to your wife and you'll be a better husband, you'll be a better daddy, and you'll be a better glorifier. That's God's plan and it works. It really, really works. Try it and see. See if it doesn't work.

A FORETASTE

Let me give you another reason to focus your energies toward your wife. This statement from John Piper will just blow your mind.

"God gave sex so we could have a language and images to understand Him better."

Got that? God gave us sex, that pleasureful physical act, so we could better understand what it means to be in a right relationship with God.

In other words, if you think sex is good, it is far more amazing to be in a right relationship with the King of kings and Lord of lords, the Lamb of God that takes away the sin of the world!

If you think that is taking it too far, we see the language of intimacy in Ezekiel, chapter 16: God takes a filthy, newborn, bloodstained Israel and cleans her up, makes her beautiful, puts jewelry on her, loves her, makes her His bride, and lavishes affection on His bride.

And what does Israel do? She goes seeking after others. And listen to the language that God uses to describe Israel and their wanderings in verse 15 of Ezekiel 16, "But thou didst trust in thine own beauty, and playedst the harlot because of thy renown, and pouredst out thy fornications on every one that passed by; his it was."

God loved Israel like a husband loves a wife; and when Israel did not love Him in return, He considered Israel an unfaithful harlot who had given herself to another. Why? Because God wanted an intimate, monogamous relationship with His children.

Verse 32-33, "But as a wife that committeth adultery, which taketh strangers instead of her husband! They give gifts to all whores: but thou givest thy gifts to all thy lovers, and hirest them, that they may come unto thee on every side for thy whoredom."

Now, if you are thinking that Israel has nothing to do with you, we are Israel, if you will. He's taken us filthy, dirty creatures and He's cleansed us through the washing of regeneration that was provided when Jesus Christ died on a cross taking upon Himself your sins and my sins so that we could be cleansed and made a beautiful bride. And every time we look at pornography, Sir, you play the whore toward your God.

Your pornography tells me how you feel about God. When you look at dirty images, you tell God, "I don't love you the way You have loved me. I am not grateful. I prefer being intimate with pixels than with you."

My friend, that is the cure to your porn problem: you need to be loving God so much, the thought of viewing porn is unimaginable. When you love God as deeply as you are supposed to, there is no way you can look at it! How could you do such a thing?

Imagine a man who was given this choice for dinner: perfectly cooked prime rib or a bowl of dog food. Now imagine the man chose the Alpo, what would you think?

I suspect you would think he was either very confused or lacking in judgment. But that is precisely what you do when you look at porn. You are choosing the lesser thing.

Your problem, in the moment you are tempted, is that you are believing the lie that says, "Porn is better than God." When you give into your lusts, you are failing to remember that God is better than prime rib; and He is certainly better than dog food. God is the best thing in the universe.

God has died for you. Redeemed you. Adopted you. Prepared a place for you. Granted you an inheritance. Ponder that deeply and I dare you to fire up your favorite website.

That is your problem; when you are viewing porn, you are forgetting God's great love for you. To view pornography is to have Gospel amnesia. Your pornography is not a physical problem; it is a spiritual problem.

When you are succumbing to the temptation to view porn, you are acting like a practical atheist. Your computer viewing habits reflect your theology and your faith. The man who loves the Lord will not desire a lesser love.

The man who is consumed by the thought of God's great love for him will not desire to play the harlot. And therein lies your cure: focus more on the Gospel, you will desire porn less.

That's your cure, Sir. There's your cure.

Grow in your gratitude for the cross, see the kindness of your God and turn your affection toward Him. Those forbidden images will soon repulse you. Tempted no more, you'll hate it. It's disgusting compared to God.

Don't wait! See what a good God He is and grow in that love for Him and you'll mortify your porn habit. Please kill it today, please! Let your self-denial show your love and gratitude for Him. Let your denial glorify Him.

The next time you are tempted, think about His bleeding on a cross for you, "Oh God, I love you way more than I love my flesh. I love you so much more, I won't do this, because I love you."

There are two other motivators that can help you in your moments of temptation: fear and rewards.

Do you want to be sitting at your computer looking at porn when your God returns to judge the world? Do you want God to discipline you? Do you not fear the Lord?

I would beg you, I beg you today, Sir, please kill it once and for all, before He kills it for you. Or before He runs out of patience and kills you. He can, you know?

God loves you enough that He might put you through something horrific to lead you to repentance. Perhaps He will have your wife or children walk in on you. Perhaps your wife will leave you. Perhaps you will lose your job, your ministry, your home.

But please know this; God would rather not punish you. God would prefer something else for you. God would actually prefer to reward you.

That's right, God would rather give you rewards

for your obedience (I Cor. 3:8). Imagine that; God has seen you at your computer and still wants to reward you for serving Him.

Sir, you have every reason in the world to stop viewing pornography. Your God loves you, died for you, and promises you Heavenly rewards. He offers you the opportunity to be a noble man who plays the role of Jesus Christ. This is an offer that only a fool can refuse. The man who chooses pornography is a fool. Don't be that man!

TWO GROUPS OF MEN

Now, I would like to talk to two groups of men. You will have to determine which group you are in.

While both of these groups claim to be followers of Jesus Christ, there is something that differentiates you from the other group.

GROUP NUMBER ONE

Once in a while you stumble and view pornography. On occasion, and I don't know how often that occasion is, this particular sin trips you up.

You battle this sin like nobodies' business. You actually take steps to have victory. You look at it less today than you did last year. When you fall, you weep bitter tears.

Group number one, I need to tell you this; the Bible does not give you definitive assurance that you are saved. I would love to say, "Absolutely, 100%. You're fine, because it's just an occasional stumble."

I have consulted with many high profile evangelicals to ask them if a man who views pornography can actually be a Christian. And frankly, they're split. Half said you can definitely be a Christian if it's an occasional fall. Others said, "Are you kidding me? That's like somebody saying, 'I only embezzled from work every three months or so.' Or, 'I only do heroin every other weekend.'" It seemed preposterous to them.

There are four considerations that must be weighed in determining the salvation of your soul:

1. The type of sin

Pornography is a wicked and perverse sin. Let me count the ways. I Corinthians 6:15-20 describes the multiple ways you sin when you connect your body with a prostitute, even if it is through a printed page or a computer screen.

Do you not know that your bodies are members of Christ? Shall I then take away the members of Christ and make them members of a pro-stitute? May it never be! [16] Or do you not know that the one who joins himself to a prostitute is one body *with her*? For He says, "The two shall become one flesh." [17] But the one who joins himself to the Lord is one spirit with *Him*. [18] Flee immorality. Every *other* sin that a man commits is outside the body, but the immoral man sins against his own body.[19] Or do you not know that your body is a temple of the Holy Spirit who is in you, whom you have from God, and that you are not your own? [20] For you have been bought with a price: therefore glorify God in your body.

➢ As a Christian, you're body is a member of the Lord Jesus Christ. When you link with a prostitute through pornography, you are bringing Jesus into your partnership.

➢ It is a violation of the covenant vow you took before God and man. You are committing the act that should be reserved exclusively for your bride.

➢ It is a profound sin against your body, unlike any other.

➢ As the temple of the Holy Spirit, you are contaminating God's temple.

➤ You are forgetting the Gospel; that you were purchased at a great price.

2. The frequency of the sin.

There are two considerations regarding the frequency of this particular sin. How often you partake and how long it takes you to commit this sin.

He that committeth sin is of the devil; for the devil sinneth from the beginning. For this purpose the Son of God was manifested, that he might destroy the works of the devil. Whosoever is born of God doth not commit sin; for his seed remaineth in him: and he cannot sin, because he is born of God" (1 John 3:8-9 KJV).

We need to understand the Greek language here. John is saying that if you continue in sin, you are of the devil. We need to remember that Christians might sin, but Christians don't "keep on sinning."

Christians fall; they don't dive. Christians don't live a willful, unrepentant lifestyle of ongoing sin. I know what you are wondering, "How often is too often to be considered a lifestyle?"

I don't know what that pattern is. Is it once a year? Once every 5 years? I don't know. That should frighten you.

The second consideration regarding the duration

of this sin is: how long does it take you to perform this sin? It is one thing to have a fleeting thought about a woman; it is another thing to plot, plan, strategize, perform your deed, and clean up the evidence.

A man who looks at porn has to make sure nobody can bust him. He must search the net for his favorite site. He must watch until he is satisfied. He must then make sure nobody can track his Internet activity. That is radically different than seeing a female form walking down the street and glancing too long.

Looking at pornography, by its very nature, might be diving into sin.

3. The earnestness of the battle

A Christian is willing to cut off his right hand if it causes him to sin. In other words, he is serious about the seriousness of sin. If you are not warring against this sin, you have every reason to be concerned about the state of your soul.

4. The response to your sin

When you complete your dirty deed, you undoubtedly feel bad. But why?

Is it because, "I feel like such a loser."

Is it because, "I just can't get victory in this area!"

Is it because, "Uh oh, if my wife walked in on this, I would be really embarrassed!"

Is it because, "If my employer found out, I might lose my job."

Is it because, "If my children found out, I would be ashamed."

That is Esau and Judas Iscariot sorrow. That is the sorrow that is motivated only because of the consequences of the sin.

If those are the reasons you feel bad, you are in danger. You are exercising mere worldly sorrow (II Cor. 7: 10-11). You are expressing the type of sorrow that leads to death.

True godly sorrow that leads to life looks very different. Godly sorrow says, "Oh God, how could I sin against you in this way? I am so sorry!"

Godly sorrow is remorse for sinning against the One who has saved you. If you have that type of godly guilt, then you might have some assurance. You might have assurance if you're willing to do anything to not sin; cut off a hand, pluck out an eye, unplug the computer, throw it out of your house, burn the books, change your job, whatever.

You're willing to do anything because you hate it so much. In fact you're even willing to disclose this to an elder at your church. Are you willing to go that far?

Why is that so important that we go to an elder if we're struggling in a sin area like this? Because they can sit down with you to help you determine if you are a stumbling, struggling child of God; or if you are a false convert who is fooling everyone including yourself.

I cannot encourage you strongly enough to confide in your pastor that you are struggling with pornography so he can walk through this with you and tell you, "Okay, you're saved, but we've got to kill this area and here is how we're going to do it."

And maybe they might discover, "You know what friend? I am very concerned that you're not saved."

Maybe they have to discipline you and set you outside of the church. Go to an elder and get help. If you're willing to do that, that is a great sign that you truly are saved and that you are struggling with this area and it is a stumble area, but it doesn't disqualify you from the Kingdom.

Incidentally, pornography is one of the greatest killers of assurance. Almost every man who has ever confided in me that he lacks assurance also views pornography. If you would like to have assurance, mortify this sin, once and for all.

GROUP NUMBER TWO

You're addicted to pornography. You don't fall, you dive into this sin. You carry it out and perhaps feel some sort of remorse, but it isn't long before you are at it again. There's no evidence that you're in a battle. There's no growth in holiness in mastering your sexual desires.

Pornography has control of you and not vice versa. There is no godly sorrow in your life, only sorrow for fear of getting caught. You're not growing in holiness, you're not in the Word every day. You will not do what it takes to kill this.

You need to be very concerned about the salvation of your soul. A good tree does not bear rotten fruit. Furthermore, if you continue in willful, unrepentant sin, the Bible says you are of the devil (I John 3:8-9).

While pornography is a problem for you, you actually have a much greater problem: you are probably not saved. You have not repented in complete humility and trusted the Savior. You do not love the Lord, you don't appreciate what He's done for you, you're not in a war, you don't battle.

Possibly you've never understood salvation; you've never understood repentance and faith. I don't know, but if something doesn't radically change, you will not spend eternity with your Master, because He is not your Master; He is your enemy. So let's address this as if your eternity depended on it; because it does.

I do not endorse Michael Pearl's ministry, but he wrote something so powerful, I'm going to share it with you because this might be exactly what you need to shock you out of your complacency. Grab onto your chairs, this might be a little bumpy.

Sir, if you isolate yourself in a room and indulge in pornography you are not sick. You are evil. You are a pervert. A real man is bigger than his lust, he is big enough to say "No" to his passions. A man whose passions are stimulated to the point of being all consuming is not a man of greater prowess, he is a man whose soul has shrunk until his perversion is the strongest thing left.

God created us with a sexual drive but He also gave us a steering wheel and a brake to direct and control our drives. If you can't control yours it is not a statement of the strength of your drive, but of the weakness of your soul. You are wasting away to the level of an alley cat. Adam fell, but you are falling even further. You're plunging your soul into eternal destruction, moving as far away from God as you can get.

You are lost, you do not deserve sympathy or understanding, you deserve condemnation and scorn. You are not a victim, you're a perpetrator. You sneak around like a thief as you lie and deceive. Your whole life is dedicated to the dragon. Your body is being consumed as your soul is being digested, you're having communion with the devil, bowing in worship of the flesh. You're a disciple of evil.

The lust you've created is never satisfied—it's an itch with no scratch, only more itch. Pornographic satisfaction is like a pot of gold at the end of the rainbow. Always just out of reach. Pornography destroys your ability to make love and replaces it with cunning wit to use and abuse. You do not deserve a woman. You have nothing to be proud of. You're not a bull, you're a dog and there are millions just like you. Some of them hang around bars, night spots, porno shops. But take note, you feed on the same diet. Your soul is a receptacle of the same putrefaction.

You might convince yourself that you're forced to your actions by an unresponsive wife, but I don't buy it. I have known pornographers that got married to good women, but found that they liked to be alone, better than sharing. Your secret world is revolting to men who know how to love women, one woman, and dedicate the rest of their energies to creative living. [1]

Ephesians 5:6 speaking of fornication, PORNIAH, in the Greek says, "Let no man deceive you with vain words: for because of these things cometh the wrath of God upon the children of disobedience." If you think you can continue indulging in pornography and still be a Christian, you are blindly hoping against the clear statements of Scripture.

Disciples of Christ read their Bibles, not dirty books! You're dangling your soul and the souls of your children over the fires of eternal damnation. I have not been as hard on you as God will be with you on the Day of Judgment.

You have only one hope: Repent toward God. You must repent toward God!

If you are still struggling, falling and doing it repeatedly with little or no remorse, you have not repented toward God, a complete coming clean before the Savior. "It is a fearful thing to fall into the hands of the living God" (Hebrews 10:31), but it is a blessed thing to stay there until you are forgiven and cleansed and then empowered to walk in holiness.

The dragon can be killed by Christ alone! You have no hope without Jesus Christ! Whom Christ makes free, he shall be free indeed! I have seen God save and deliver lesbians, homosexuals, pornography addicts as easily as He saves chaste youths. Christ is sufficient and He will save, but you must come clean today! Now, now! Kill it or He will crush you!

Do you understand His goodness? How holy He is and how perfect He is and what He will do with you on the Day of Judgment, if you do not have it cleansed from your slate? Do you know what a trashing you are in for, Sir? Is hell hot? Unimaginably hot, because your sin is so filthy and offensive to a high and holy God.

This day He will save you if you fall before Him in repentance. You are in a time of grace. He will save you this day to the uttermost. Do not delay. Run to your Savior. Run.

Your cup of wrath will one day be filled to the brim and God will demand you drink it to the dregs. But…

But God is rich in mercy; and He loves you with such great love that He sent His Son to drink your cup of wrath so you don't have to.

God took your filth, perversions, fantasies and self-pleasuring and laid those and all of your sins on His spotless Son. Jesus took your shame, your vile, nasty, dirty, disgusting sins and owned them as His own…for you. For you.

God then poured out the justice that you deserve for your sins on Jesus so you don't have to be punished for being the criminal you are.

What did Jesus endure for you? He was punched

in the face until He was so disfigured, you could not even tell He was a human being. For you.

He was stripped naked and mocked by soldiers. For you.

He was whipped with a cat-o-nine tails. For you.

He had nails banged through His feet and hands. For you.

He gasped for breath while His shredded back rubbed against rough timber. For you.

He died. For you.

If you will repent and trust Jesus this day, He will forgive your sins, take away your guilt and remove your shame.

Then He will give you the power to slay the lust dragon. You cannot slay it on your own. You lose to him every time because you have no power. But God is stronger than your lusts, and the same Holy Spirit who gave Jesus the power to resist temptation will grant you the same power.

Your lusts will not stop shouting at you, but God will increasingly deliver you from the power of pornography. And you will become the man your wife longs for you to be. You will become the Daddy that your children think you are.

Stop putting your children's souls in jeopardy. Stop crushing your wife. And if you think she doesn't know, then you are an even bigger fool. She knows and she's been praying for this day and she's been praying for this moment.

But don't make the mistake that so many men make. Pornographers tend to think that the totality of their problem is just this one sin. It is not. You have a much bigger problem than lust.

You need to grasp the totality of your sin nature. The Bible says that all liars will have their part in a lake of fire, because every lie is an abomination to a holy God.

What about everything you've taken that didn't belong to you? Does God keep tabs? Meticulously. Perhaps you think this sounds silly. Oh, God is not being silly. He is high and holy and perfect. And if you take a paper clip, He sees you as a thief. He is not impressed with the value of the object. He sees you as a liar, as an adulterer, as a pornographer, or as a blasphemer if you take His name in vain.

If you do not love the Lord with all of your heart, soul, mind and strength, then you are an idolater. What you have done against a high and holy God deserves His anger and His wrath and He will pour it out on you on the Day of Judgment. He will grind you to powder.

Don't think that you have a sin problem because you look at porn; you have a sin problem because you are a sinner.

Let me ask you a question; what would you do with a dog that repeatedly bit your hand when you tried to feed him? What would you do with a dog who never came when you called? What would you do with a dog who constantly trashed your home?

You and I are that dog. You and I justly deserve God's temporal and eternal punishment.

But God, to demonstrate His kindness, sent forth His Son, born of a virgin, to live under the law to redeem those of us under the curse of the law. He was beaten, He died on a cross, shed His blood. He rose from the dead and He is ascended into Heaven where He sits at the right hand of the Father and He stands ready to be your High Priest and your intercessor.

He stands willing to forgive you, a pornographer, a liar, a blasphemer.

His patience with you will not last forever. One day, He will end your life and call you to judgment. Or, at His appointed time, He will return to earth with His holy angels in flaming fire to judge the earth in righteousness. If you are found without His righteousness He will destroy you.

Flee to Him now! Flee to Him now before His patience runs out and He comes after you! Flee to Him! You should be horrified of hell; it is hot and it goes on for forever and ever. Please, turn to the

Savior, not because you're afraid of hell but turn to Him because He's been so kind to save you from hell!

Why would you delay? If I could get on my face before you and beg you, I would. If I could repent for you I would do it for you. I can't. Nobody can do it.

You, Sir, go before God and think of your sins. Let it crush you, bury you, and trouble you. Let it make you fearful and then, when you can hardly breathe, turn and look at the blood-stained cross where Jesus Christ, God Himself, died for you and it will break your heart. It will lead you, not to a worldly sorrow that leads to death, but a godly sorrow that leads to life.

Gaze at your holy God on the cross hanging there for you, the pornographer. Stare at Jesus the merciful, ready and willing to forgive, save and cleanse you.

Consider how God describes sin; this is what God sees in us. Sin to God is the scum of a seething pot in which is a detestable carcass. It is the blood and pollution of a newborn child. Sin to God is a dead and rotting body. It is the foul stench of the fumes that come from an opening of a tomb. God sees our sins as the lust of the devil.

And yet, He loves us. Do you fathom the kindness? All we do, day in and day out, is shake our fist and sin against Him and violate His noble plans for us and do our filthy, selfish things and He says, "I love you anyway."

How does God see sin? God sees sin in the most horrible, horrible, horrible state. He sees it as a putrefying source. Our sins are like a menstrual cloth. Our sins are like a canker or gangrene before God. Our sins are the dung of filthy creatures. Our sins are the vomit of a dog.

But God says, "I love you anyway."

Why would you reject this God? Why would you not want to be in a right relationship with a God who is rich in mercy? Why would you not want to live forever with a God who died for your sins, all of your sins?

Repent and trust Jesus. For God so loved the world that He gave His only begotten Son that whoever believes in Him will not perish but have everlasting life. God demonstrated His love for us by dying for us while we were yet sinners.

What are you going to do, Sir? What are you going to do? What are you waiting for? What is needed? What sort of sermon needs to be preached?

What do you want from God? What more does He need to do for you? What is it going to take? What does your God need to do for you? Die for you?

God has given you everything, absolutely everything. He has given His Son to die for your sins so you can go to heaven when He should have given you hell.

Call out to Him. Now is the right time. He will hear you! Do not reject this marvelous message of His amazing kindness!

Don't put your head on your pillow tonight without first getting on your face before God!

Jesus is good! Jesus is kind! Jesus is merciful. Jesus will save! Repent and let Him save you! Today is the day of salvation!

BIBLIOGRAPHY

1 Pearl, Michael, *Pornography — The Road To Hell,* No Greater Joy Ministry, Pleasantville, TN, 2001